NICE THINGS
ABOUT
GROWING OLDER

by William Wiswall Meyer

Cover design by Terry Schultz.

NICE THINGS ABOUT GROWING OLDER
by William Wiswall Meyer

Copyright © 1990
Educational Ministries, Inc.

ISBN 1-877871-11-7

EDUCATIONAL MINISTRIES, INC.
2861-C Saturn Street
Brea, CA 92621

CONTENTS

INTRODUCTION

There are many NICE THINGS ABOUT GROWING OLDER and some of them are mentioned in these pages. Why didn't I include BAD things, and give a more balanced account? Simply because too many people have talked at length about the bad things.

This is not a treatise on aging, and there is no logical sequence in the readings. A few are seasonal, but there is no chronology. Each page is a unit, a simple meditation.

Many books about growing older speak in the third person about aging, because most of them seem to be written by gerontologists in their fifties or forties or thirties, who have never been there yet. So they talk about "them." In these meditations I talk about us!

By contrast, many of the great classics about spirituality and creative living were written by elders who rightly regarded their chronological age as irrelevant to spiritual insight.

When is "older"? We're about as young (or old) as we feel. In 1776 the life span of Americans was said to be about 48 years. By 1900 it was around 50. Now it has zoomed to at least 76, and is still going up, thanks to modern medicine. Some gerontologists even refer to younger elders (60-70), middle elders (70-80) and elder elders (over 85). But you and I have known some 92 year olds who think and act younger than some 62 year olds. Chronological age is not our master and not our limit, as these pages will testify.

Many books about growing older decry "ageism," which is prejudice or discrimination on account of age. But some of them, while trying to be upbeat, slip back into the agism they decry by assuming that everyone over 60 is declining or afraid of declining, and is haunted by the fear of death. As one who is now 75 I say that's humbug. Of course there are elders who are sick in body or in mind. So also there are teenagers who are afflicted with cancer, AIDS, schizophrenia, drug addiction, suicidal urges, and even progeria. Yet few people would say "How sad to be a teenager." Somehow Americans idolize youth in spite of the afflictions teens are prone to.

Many studies about aging have been written, including learned statistics and questionnaires. There are also guidebooks such as Eugene Bianchi's excellent "Aging as a Spiritual Adventure" and his "On Growing Older." Instead, this little book just tries to "accentuate the positive" and to lift up some things many forget or underestimate.

This is not just another book of devotions, although these meditations have already been used in many groups of elders. Originally they were shared in a Senior Day Care center, and the careful reader may notice a few references to such a setting, which included frail elderly victims of strokes, Alzheimer's, Parkinson's, along with the active elderly volunteers who shared with them their hours and their love.

Only about 5% of America's elders are in so-called rest homes, although perhaps 20% are seriously handicapped in some way. The other 80% are or should be enjoying elderhood, as Browning described it:

"Grow old along with me:
The best is yet to be,
The last of life for which the first was made."

As Young As We Feel

ONE OF THE NICE THINGS ABOUT GROWING OLDER is that we can still be about as young as we feel.

On my sixtieth birthday I entitled my sermon: "I Don't Remember Growing Older." That's a phrase from the poignant "Sunrise, Sunset" in Fiddler on the Roof. I think the experience is important. I feel that I'm the same person I was when I was 40 or 30 or 20. I am a person who is not fully tied to this body and this chronology. Now that I'm 75 I feel it just as much, and I'm a bit surprised every time I look in a mirror and see that fellow with all the white hair!

Meister Eckhart puts it very strongly when he talks about the youthfulness of the soul. In sermon 8 he said, "Understand that my soul is as young as it was when it was created. Indeed, it is even younger! And understand that it would not surprise me if it were younger tomorrow than today."

George Burns was interviewed on his 90th birthday. "Mr. Burns, is it true you go out with young girls?" "Yes." "Mr. Burns, is it true you smoke 15 to 20 cigars a day?" "Yes." "Mr. Burns, is it true you drink 5 martinis a day?" "Yes." "What does your doctor say to all this?" "My doctor's dead."

Katharine Hepburn was recently asked how at age 75 she keeps her vitality. She replied that the secret to her youthful glow and inner happiness is vitality. "Lack of vitality is a terrible lack. It can mean that you just don't try." Four time Academy Award winner actress, Hepburn said she loves getting down on her hands and knees and communing with the earth. "My hands are strong. I can sift and get out the old crab-grass roots and dump in the topsoil and humus and peat and manure and mix them with the sand. I can crawl through the flower bed and weed... Limited vitality, certainly, but better than nothing."

God help us to keep our vitality and to get some fun out of life today and everyday.

God Accepts Us Now

ONE OF THE NICE THINGS ABOUT GROWING OLDER is that we can at last understand that God accepts us as we are, even though God is constantly nudging us to do better! God forgives our failures and renews our lease on life, to the extent that we also forgive others and grant them life.

Meister Eckhart in one of the most remarkable paragraphs (R. Blakney translation, p. 18) says "Indeed, once we are set in the will of God, one will not wish that the sin he committed had never happened. To be sure, it was contrary to God, but by it he is committed to greater love, being abased and humbled because he did act contrary to the will of God. You may, however, fully trust God not to have put the sin upon you, except to bring out the best that is in you. Thus when you rise above sin and turn away from it, God, who is faithful, will act as if you had never sinned at all and not for a moment will He let the former sins count against you.

"Even if your sins were as great in number as all mankind's put together, still He would not count them against you and He would still have as much confidence in you as He ever had in any creature. If only God finds you ready, He will pay no attention to what you were before. God is God of the present; as He finds a man, so God takes him and accepts him, not for what he has been but for what he is now.

"One seldom hears of people achieving great things without first making mistakes. It is our Lord's intention that thus we shall learn how great His compassion is, and be warned to greater humility and devotion."

Such is the mystery of God's forgiveness. God, help us to forgive others, that we in turn may find forgiveness.

Our Love Shall Conquer

ONE OF THE NICE THINGS ABOUT GROWING OLDER is to be outgoing and accepting to everyone who comes to us. Our loving fellowship helps to melt down our own barriers, and the barriers that others may set up. I remember the sign over the hearth of an old English Inn:

HAIL GUEST! If friend, we welcome thee.
If stranger, no longer be.
If foe, our love shall conquer thee!

Our outgoing love is in the last analysis the only thing that can outmaneuver enmity. Edwin Markham put the strategy in a classic quatrain:

"He drew a circle to shut me out;
Heretic, rebel, a thing to flout;
But love and I had the wit to win;
We drew a circle that took him in!"

Bergson says there's a difference not in degree but in kind between a we vs. they feeling and a universal we feeling which includes everyone. Some folks are shy and need to work at being outgoing. But we can work at it. We need reminding that God's love, if it is to include us, must include everyone else too. Sometimes it takes a bit of heroism to forget ourselves and just think of others. Here's a very dramatic story to remind us of that heroism:

Back in the days before helicopters, when a team of men in a giant rowboat launched out through the surf to rescue ships, a young Coast Guard recruit was on duty in his first big storm. Then came the whistle of a ship in distress, and the Captain prepared to launch the lifeboat in the seething waves. The young recruit shouted and grabbed his arm: "Captain, we can't go out in this storm. We'd never get back alive." The old captain turned and said: "Our job is to go out. We don't have to come back."

That's an extreme case. But thank God there are many quiet heroes who forget themselves and their own safety to save others. The risk of friendship is an everyday challenge to get out of our own self-centeredness, to see the needs of those around us, to draw a circle that takes in all of God's children. God help us to have the courage everyday to love others as much as we love ourselves.

We Can Take It

ONE OF THE NICE THINGS ABOUT GROWING OLDER is to be able to take a bit of abuse and laugh it off.

I'm thinking now of what they call "ageism": prejudice against seniors, ignoring older persons, discounting our abilities, bypassing us for any appointment or nomination, putting us on the shelf, and so on. I say we just have to laugh it off. We have to develop thick skins. We have to prove our worth to ourselves, and then either convince them or ignore them!

Although "elder abuse" is now a recognized phenomenon which includes physical abuse and legal and financial maneuvering, abuse is very widespread. At any age or station in life, we have to learn to stand up for our own rights, and to stand up for each other.

We also have to learn to "take it" if we want to survive emotionally. We have to learn the technique of returning a smile for a sneer, by feeling truly sorry for the person whose lifestyle is the swagger and the sneer.

If we go on to learn the art of returning good for evil, we're almost getting Christian! "If your enemy hungers, feed him. If he's thirsty give him a drink. It will drive him crazy." (Romans 12:20, paraphrased)

We're getting close to the strategy of living in the shadow of the cross. Like the young martyr who stood before King Henry of Navarre and said: "Sire, you can kill me, but you cannot kill my Church. For it may please your Majesty to know that the Church of Jesus Christ, which I have the honor to represent today, is an anvil that has worn out many hammers!"

That's a bit more dramatic than the kinds of "abuse" we usually get as seniors in a society that worships youth. We aren't going to call ourselves martyrs, but we might call ourselves shock absorbers. Autos were a lot more bumpy before the shock absorber came along. It takes sharp knocks and levels them out into pleasant ripples. It returns good for evil. Every family needs at least one shock absorber for this world of hard knocks in which we all live. God help us today and everyday to return a smile for a sneer, to make life easier for ourselves as well as for others.

Pass It On

ONE OF THE NICE THINGS ABOUT GROWING OLDER is that we have time to think about what we are going to pass on to the next generations. And I don't mean just real estate or money, or even antiques and family mementoes. I mean a heritage of trust and love and steadfastness.

Psychologist Eric Erickson labels this aspect of later life as "Generativity": the concern for the coming generations, calling forth our best creativity. In some cultures, such as ancient Chinese and Jewish, the elders were venerated and needed. It was their function to cherish and to pass on the traditions, and the younger generations listened respectfully. In our American and increasingly in world culture, we oldsters tend to be ignored or at best tolerated. Margaret Mead has warned us of this danger to the transmission of culture. It is caused in part by technology changing so rapidly that the generation gap has become a chasm, and the generations can hardly communicate. But communicate we must; it's part of our very nature. Generativity means that we must take the initiative.

Perhaps the doll cradle and the Noah's Ark and the rocking horse I have made for my own grandchildren will last and be handed down longer than the ideas and ideals I have tried to share with them. I sometimes wonder. But I am confident that some of my love of nature and my love of people and love of God has rubbed off on these youngsters. I think that my concern for planet earth and for world peace and brotherhood, some of my love for great music and great books, has gotten through to them too. I remember now how much I learned about plants and about gardening from my parents, although I didn't do any gardening until I had a garden of my own. I like to feel that my dad would be proud to see my garden today, to know that his generativity wasn't wasted!

Then let's keep thinking: what shall we pass on to the next generations? Right now in the history of humankind, the most important thing is the very chance to survive — the very continuity of life on the planet earth. That sounds ominous. And it is ominous that life on earth could be extinguished in a few hours or days, if the wrong buttons were pushed! God help us to use our prayers and our lives to keep the world together, that all of the blessings we have received from the past may be handed on unscathed.

Slightly "As Is"

ONE OF THE NICE THINGS ABOUT GROWING OLDER is that we can accept each other just as we are. We don't have to worry or to pretend. All we have to do is to be sure that we accept others, as we want to be accepted.

Recently I've been reading another book that discusses symptoms of some of our most mysterious diseases, because I try to keep as informed as I can in order to better help people. But I'm very glad that we don't have to talk about symptoms and diagnoses. We can leave that to the doctors. We can accept each other just as we are. That's a big enough challenge!

I'm reminded of a fine china shop that had a discount table marked "AS IS." The customer examined a lovely vase and finally asked the clerk why it was on the discount table. "Well, sir," was the reply, "That one is only slightly as is." If we are along in years and apparently healthy we may be referred to as "well preserved," but I much prefer the label "only slightly as is."

I remember one old friend who, when confronted with the traditional "Good morning, how are you?" would reply "Pretty good, for the shape I'm in!" Another retort is "Do you really want to hear?"

To accept each other just as we are means we must be open and sincere. And sometimes we can even joke about our limitations with no offense. Paul said to the Romans (Ch. 12) "Let your love be sincere," but an older version says "Let your love be without hypocrisy." The word "sincere" comes from the fine china shops in Roman days. A shrewd seller of pottery, finding a piece with a crack, found that he could fill it with wax. After a bit of polish, the piece might get by the unwary eye of the buyer and get a full price. Honest merchants began putting up signs that said "SINE CERE", which is Latin for "Without wax", no pretense, no hypocrisy. The practice became so traditional that the word is with us: SINCERE — no cover-up, no disinformation, no false front.

We may be slightly as is, but let's be without wax, accepting each other just as we are, as we want to be accepted.

Let's Keep Growing

ONE OF THE NICE THINGS ABOUT GROWING OLDER is that we can, if we will, adjust to big changes that are happening in the world.

Quite a few studies show that middle-aged folks are more conservative than older folks, and that sometimes oldsters can understand and be sympathetic with teenagers better than the middle-aged can. Somebody says it this way — that it's more fun to be a grandparent than a parent.

Changes in the world are coming faster, it seems, with every generation that goes by, due to the rapid advances in science and technology and their rapid disbursement into the life of the world.

Jack Smith recently told about taking his grandson out to buy him a pair of shoes. He finally paid $52 for a pair of Adidas, and he remembered that a good pair of tennis shoes cost around $4 when he was 15. He went on to comment, though, that in 1931 when people with a good job earned perhaps $25 a week, to pay $4 then seemed more than paying $52 now. I guess it's the dollar that changed.

Recently when I went to Boise, my plane was late, and when I strolied around the L.A. airport I saw that a $.05 ice cream cone costs $1.85 and a $.10 milkshake is now $2.50 and I'll bet it isn't as big or as thick as they used to be! But continuing inflation is merely one small example of change we must face.

Times change, but they always have and they always will. It is the creative response of life to grow, to adapt, to meet changing conditions with courage and faith and joy. But I still don't use a computer!

God help us to keep growing all our lives, to reach out to new possibilities, and so to be survivors.

Invited To A Party

ONE OF THE NICE THINGS ABOUT GROWING OLDER is that we can be invited to a party. Once a friend of mine wrote about life as a party to which we're all invited. She began by remembering the prodigal son who had been seeking only his selfish pleasure. Then he "came to himself" and saw his life was a mess and he decided to return home, for home was like heaven in comparison to where he was now. The father was so happy that the son had found himself that he said, "Let's have a party." But the older son was jealous and didn't want to come, because he didn't understand what his brother had gone through. Although he had enjoyed the blessings of being with his father all along, he didn't really appreciate them. (Do we ever take love for granted?)

"As a teenager," Marge continues, "I came to the conclusion that life was a mess. I saw competitive, self-centered, materialistic attitudes — people trying to put themselves up by putting others down. Then I discovered that Jesus loves all people so much that he was willing to give his life to show that the way to life is through loving and caring, just as God loves each of us."

Through the centuries we have worked hard at trying to make Jesus only "a man of sorrows." Read the Gospels again and see that he was criticized as "a glutton and a drunkard, a friend of tax collectors and sinners." His Kingdom is abundant joy for all.

So, life can be a party, and Jesus invites us. It's a come-as-you-are party and there are no admission requirements, except that we want to share God's love and joy with open hearts with everyone who comes. Let's remember that it is more than an ordinary party...it's forever!

Unfinished Business

ONE OF THE NICE THINGS ABOUT GROWING OLDER is that we can have a lot of unfinished business and not get too upset about it.

All my life I've kept lists of things I ought to do or want to do. They used to bother me. Of course I got more things done with a bit of prodding and reminding.

Now that I'm retired I try to do things one at a time and not make lists, although there may be a few still hidden away in my desk. Today's shopping list can be thrown away before suppertime.

My first boss gave me some good advice: "You're the kind of person who will always see more things to do than you ever have time to do. Be sure you do the most important things first, even if you have to let some things go." But now we can often just do what we want to do, with no compulsions.

I think it was Robert Browning who said,
"A man's reach must exceed his grasp,
Else what's a heaven for."

This means we must reach out even for plans that we know will never be completed in our own lifetime. When I visited the parsonage where my own grandfather used to live in Kohala, Hawaii, I saw a beautiful palm tree over 100 feet tall. Family photos from 1895 showed that tree only 5 ft. high; it had been planted for generations yet to be born! Remember the builders of medieval cathedrals who knew it could take centuries to finish them.

So I remember that having Unfinished Business is a very important part of being human. It can mean looking beyond the calendar of our own days, beyond the horizon of our present lives. Longing for goodness beyond our grasp is divine as well as human. God help us to keep reaching out for world peace, for harmony between races, for a good life for the whole human family!

God's Power Welling Up

ONE OF THE NICE THINGS ABOUT GROWING OLDER is that, precisely because our own physical powers become more or less limited, we can more readily feel God's Power welling up within us. I know that some of us are especially aware that each day is a gift of God and that we are granted this particular day to live by power beyond our own.

When we were younger and perhaps more strong physically, we were tempted to believe we were "self-made" men and women—although that was strictly an illusion. But now that we're older and perhaps with waning physical powers, we can recognize that life is a gift, a miracle that God performs within us and through us, moment by moment. If you don't believe me, try right now to make your heart beat! Life does it through us. God does it.

Paul the Apostle knew this from experience, because of his own serious disability (perhaps epilepsy), which he mentions many times. In II Cor. 12 he says: "A thorn was given me in the flesh, to harass me, to keep me from being too elated. The Lord said to me, 'My grace is sufficient for you, for my power is made perfect in weakness.' I will all the more gladly BOAST OF MY WEAKNESSES, that the power of Christ may rest upon me. For the sake of Christ, then, I am content with weaknesses, for when I am weak, then I am strong."

In I Cor. 2 Paul says: "I was with you in weakness and in much fear and trembling...that your faith might not rest in the wisdom of men but in the power of God." And in II. Cor. 4 Paul says: "We have God's treasure in earthen vessels, to show that the transcendent power belongs to God and not to us."

Muriel Lester was told as a teenager that she might be an invalid all her life. But as she learned to pray, she learned to "lean on the Everlasting Arms" of Divine Power. She not only recovered physically, but all of her long and blessed life she helped others to rely on God's power for healing and reconciliation. In Jesus' famous interview with the woman at the well in Samaria, he promised that the power of the Spirit, "like a well springing up into Life Eternal," is available to us.

God help us to remember that the power of the Spirit is life within us.

Laugh Your Way to Health

ONE OF THE NICE THINGS ABOUT GROWING OLDER is that we can laugh at the same old jokes more than once. I notice that we like to sing the old familiar songs over again too, better than new ones.

They tell about a group of prisoners who survived partly by telling their favorite jokes. They got so used to the jokes they had them all numbered, so somebody could just call out "#10" and everyone would laugh.

We often sing "Red Sails in the Sunset." I remember the Indian who got rich and bought his boys a yacht so he could have red sons in the sail set. And the young men who inherited a cattle ranch from their father and named it FOCUS because that's where the sun's rays meet. (The sons raise meat.)

I was brought up hearing my dad's arsenal of jokes. He never forgot a new one, but when a new audience came along they were likely to get reruns of his old favorites. Years later I realized that, as a dentist in the days when novocaine was used only in extreme cases, he used humor as a technique for helping his patients ignore their aches and pains!

Norman Cousins makes quite a program out of humor as therapy. He tells how he recovered from a serious heart attack, partly through humor. He even rented all the old comic movies and saw them again and again.

We enjoy the old Laurel and Hardy comics even though we've seen them many times before. We get laughs, and it's good therapy too.

So as we grow older, let's think of our sense of humor as one of the great blessings of life and let's enjoy each day together.

Forgiving and Forgiven

ONE OF THE NICE THINGS ABOUT GROWING OLDER is that we can forgive and we can be forgiven.

Forgiveness is a universal need because none of us is perfect. We all make mistakes sometimes, and say the wrong thing and hurt someone we love. Sometimes I come through sounding mean and ornery when I don't intend it at all. Then I need forgiveness.

Forgiveness for an occasional mean or angry word is possible when underneath we know that love binds us together. So forgiveness is a major ingredient of love.

Forgiveness has to be very specific, from one person to another, but it doesn't always have to be verbalized. When after some hurt we say, "Oh, that's O.K.," it really means, "Yes, I feel hurt but I forgive you because I love you."

The most difficult phrase in the Lord's Prayer is the petition "Forgive us, AS we forgive." Jesus goes on to warn us specifically that if we don't forgive then we can't be forgiven! This means, I think, that if we keep a barrier of resentment against someone else, then we have made a barrier that shuts us out from forgiveness for our own mistakes.

Critics sometimes accuse Christians of acting as though we are better than other people. But this is not so if we are truly Christian. For then we know very well our own faults and weaknesses and we admit them humbly. But we also know that we are accepted by God and forgiven — if we also forgive others for their sins against us. One interesting definition of the Church is "the fellowship of the forgiven." May that spirit always be a description of our church.

Accepting Spiritual Riches

ONE OF THE NICE THINGS ABOUT GROWING OLDER is that we have spiritual riches in our very grasp, if only we reach out to accept them.

It is said that we are like a man who owns a vast cellar full of rare wines, but we have forgotten they are there and have not even tasted them yet.

Or we are like a King who does not realize that he is a king and has a Kingdom at his very fingertips.

The Kingdom of God is among us, around us, within us, said Jesus. And he meant that God has given us all these treasures of the spirit by God's very act of creation, which God renews in every moment of time.

Younger folks, full of ambition and sometimes even selfishness, are usually so busy trying to build their own little private kingdoms that they often forget the infinite power and love and joy that is their birthright as children of God.

But the fence we build, or try to build, around our private kingdom is the same fence that shuts us away from God's infinite Kingdom. When we take down our fences we discover that we "own" all the beauty and love in the world, exactly because we don't try to claim it as our private possession.

Put it another way—love can never be ours if we try to possess love, for love by its very nature is shared. It happens only when we give it away with no claims or conditions—otherwise it isn't love but only possessiveness, which is the opposite of love.

Of course it isn't a matter of age. Oldsters can be selfish, and people can wake up to God's Kingdom at any moment in time. But when we're old we have less to lose, more to gain, and we now have time to realize these wonders of God's Kingdom around us and within us now. God help us today to live in the Kingdom!

The Acid Test of Faith

ONE OF THE NICE THINGS ABOUT GROWING OLDER is that we can learn to love God for Himself and not just for the things God gives us.

As youngsters we learned to say thank you for very specific things, and that's important to remember. Then we began slowly to learn that our most important thanks is not for things at all but for the "gifts of the Spirit" as Paul called our spiritual blessings.

Meister Eckhart poked fun at us when he said "Some people want...to love God as they love their cow—they love their cow for the milk and cheese and profit it makes for them. This is how it is with people who love God for the sake of outward wealth or inward comfort. They do not rightly love God when they love Him for their own advantage." (Blakney, p. 241)

To give thanks to God even in times of spiritual "dryness" when no blessings seem to come, is even harder to learn. A boy in London during World War II was asked to define austerity and he said "Austerity is being thankful for what we haven't got!"

The prophet Habakkuk put it in a beautiful poem, based on his own experience in time of famine:

"Even though the fig trees do not blossom,
Nor fruit be on the vines;
Though the produce of the olive fail
And the fields yield no food;
Though the flock be cut off from the fold
And there be no herd in the stalls,
Yet I will rejoice in the Lord,
And I will joy in the God of my salvation."   (Habakkuk 3:17-18)

I call this the Acid Test of Faith!!

God help us to be thankful for all good things and thankful for "inward comfort," but most of all to thank God for being God and always to love God for Himself above all created things.

A Beautiful Natural Happening

ONE OF THE NICE THINGS ABOUT GROWING OLDER is that we can look upon our own death, whenever it comes, as a beautiful and a natural happening. God grant to each of us a peaceful and a lovely "crossing of the bar."

Tonight, as I write these lines, I recall the epitaph Robert Louis Stevenson wrote for himself:

> "Under the wide and starry sky
> Dig the grave and let me lie.
> Glad did I live, and gladly die,
> And I laid me down with a will.
>
> "This be the verse you grave for me:
> Here he lies, where he longed to be.
> Home is the sailor, home from sea,
> And the hunter, home from the hill."

That's a lovely and moving poem, although my own wish is to have my body cremated and my ashes scattered on some mountain, so no one can find a spot and say "there he is." No, he won't be there at all: he will have joined the "choir invisible." He will have gone to add his voice to the waterfalls and the anthems of the birds and the music of the spheres.

My own prayer—and I hope it's yours too—is that we may invest and bestow and merge our lives in the common good of all humanity, in the living communion of spirits here in God's Kingdom on earth, that although we may be missed when we leave this place, our love and our spirit may be felt and understood and realized by those who live after us.

This is a heritage and indeed a presence that generations yet to come may well be proud of. But they will be strengthened and ennobled in fact, whether they understand it or not. We don't need the credit any more than we need a gravestone! God help us to live each day so we may leave behind us a heritage of love and faith.

Share Our Amazement

ONE OF THE NICE THINGS ABOUT GROWING OLDER is that we can share our amazement at the miracles of modern science and technology.

The other night after the U.S. Secretary of State said something about South Africa, the news reporter via satellite got South Africa's Foreign Minister on TV and asked him to comment in the sight and hearing of millions of Americans. I'm not commenting now on what was said, but only on the miracle of communication. When you and I were young Maggie, or even middle aged, no such thing could even be imagined!

I do have the feeling that when people even of sharply differing views can talk together, we all have a better chance of surviving together. When we discover we live in a global village, it helps to make us more sensitive and compassionate toward our distant neighbors as well as our neighbors nearby.

When I go wilderness camping with my son (who is a Ph.D. Physicist), he laughs when I look up to watch a speeding jet crossing the sunset sky. To him it's commonplace, but to me it's still amazing because I remember when there were no big planes at all, let alone jets at 37,000 feet leaving contrail clouds in the sunset sky.

You and I are often impatient with our aches and pains. But we can remember when there was no penicillin, no CAT Scans, no radiation therapy, almost no cures at all, that we take for granted today. Thank God for modern medicine, and for research still going on day after day.

Creation itself is amazing. And the older we get the more we can find new things to amaze us and to help us, and to give us cause for thanksgiving.

Expressing Affection

ONE OF THE NICE THINGS ABOUT GROWING OLDER is that we can express affection to each other without having our motives misunderstood.

We do a lot of hugging in our fellowship these days, and once in a while we kiss too. It's an expression of real affection and it's a good thing. (Especially for people who have lost the ability to speak clearly, touching and hugging are very important ways to communicate.)

When I was a youngster of 40 or 45 I would have been more than a little uneasy. I was so busy then trying to be respectable, as I understood it.

Of course you and I grew up in an era when hugging and kissing just was not done in public, even by husbands and wives. Things have changed a lot. Maybe about 20 years ago hugging became acceptable if not almost mandatory—at least in some groups and subcultures. Now it is well nigh universal.

Anyway, when we grow old we can get away with a lot more things. In many ways we have a lot more freedom, but we must use our freedom "to guard each one's dignity and save each one's pride," and never use our freedom selfishly.

So let's keep on expressing the love and affection we feel for each other. Let's keep on celebrating—not only holidays and birthdays, but everyday as we share our lives with each other.

Blest be the tie that binds
Our hearts in Christian love.
The fellowship of kindred minds
Is like to that above.

We share each other's woes,
Each other's burdens bear,
And often for each other flows
The sympathizing tear.

When we are called to part
It gives us inward pain,
But we shall still be joined in heart
And hope to meet again.

23

The Past Cannot Be Taken Away

ONE OF THE NICE THINGS ABOUT GROWING OLDER is that we have had many good experiences, and whether we remember the details or not, they cannot be taken away from us.

Maslow calls the great experiences in our lives "Peak Experiences," especially those mountain-top experiences that make us feel at one with Life and the Universe. Carl Jung says that experience is the essence of religion and cannot be disputed; "Religious experience is absolute." "They" can say, "I've never had an experience of God" but YOU can say "I have." That's a fact that stands on its own.

In a more general way, we sometimes review our lives — they say that in a moment of crisis it all passes before us! — and we are strengthened by these memories and events that add up to a back log of spiritual strength.

Victor Frankl, in counseling older persons, likewise dwells on the truth that THE PAST CANNOT BE TAKEN AWAY FROM US. "Everything is stored as though it were safely deposited in a storehouse. The past is the safest mode of being. What is past has been saved and rescued by us into the past." (V. Frankl, The Will to Meaning, p.120). In an interview with an 80 year old suffering from inoperable cancer, Frankl asks: "What do you think when you look back on your life? HAS LIFE BEEN WORTH LIVING?"

Frau Anastasia Kotek: "Well, Doctor, I must say that I had a good life. Life was nice, indeed. I must thank the Lord for what it held for me...for the grace of all of these wonderful experiences, I am grateful to the Lord."

Frankl: "(I wanted to wrestle with my patient's repressed existential despair)...do you think anyone can undo the happiness you have lived?"

Anastasia: "No, Doctor, nobody can blot it out!"

Frankl: "You have made the best of your suffering. You have become an example for all of our patients." (Students applaud!)

Anastasia: "My life is not in vain."

We Depend On Each Other

ONE OF THE NICE THINGS ABOUT GROWING OLDER is that we can freely and openly admit that we are dependent on others for our life and our welfare.

The so-called self-made man is a phony: there is simply no such thing. Sometimes we imagine that we are independent, but it's only an illusion: we belong to each other.

Just pick up a bite of lettuce and remind yourself how many people you can depend on. The grocery clerk, the wholesaler, a series of truck drivers, the grower, the cultivator, the picker, the irrigators, the builders of canals, the builders of tractors. And who made the fork and napkin and plate? We depend on others for our very lives.

It is often called one of the bad things about growing older, that we have to depend on others. It's true for all humans, but in youth and middle age folks try to deny their dependence. Tiny babies need stroking as much as they need food in order to grow up truly human. Adults do too!

I remember the day over 30 years ago, when I sat in the back seat and let my son drive the car with the whole family along. I knew that he was as good a driver as I was. (My wife might say that's not much of a compliment.) Actually I was rejoicing that I could begin to take a back seat and that I could depend on others. It was and still is a very good feeling.

The feeling of dependence or independence is a spiritual question, not even a sociological or psychological one. Independence is an illusion, but the myth may cause much of the alienation, loneliness, fear and frustration we sometimes consider our normal human fate. The feeling of dependence, our true human condition in which we can and should rejoice, seems degrading to some. It punctures our ego, but ego must be deflated before we can grow into truly loving relationships.

God help us to grow a little bit today in understanding and appreciating our dependence on others. And thank them when we can!

Enjoy Life Today

ONE OF THE NICE THINGS ABOUT GROWING OLDER is that we can have fun right now, today, and let other people worry about tomorrow and yesterday.

In the TV show "The Incredible Hulk," David Bonner falls in love with a lady doctor who has a fatal disease and only a short time to live. He proposes marriage, but she says they don't have enough time. He tells her this story:

Once upon a time, a man was being chased by a tiger and he came to the edge of a cliff. Looking backward he saw the tiger approach, so he jumped. On the way down, he reached out and grabbed a bush and was saved. He looked down and saw another tiger waiting at the bottom of the cliff, smacking its lips. Just as he felt the bush begin to weaken, he noticed a wild strawberry growing out of a crack in the rocky cliff. With one hand, he reached out and picked the strawberry and ate it. And he said to himself, "Now, that is a delicious strawberry." And that is just how it is with us!

Life, they say, is a terminal illness. From the day we're born we know some day we will die, and we never know when it will be. Some of us have been told we have a serious illness, but it goes for all of us even if we feel well now. But in the course of human history, the moment in which we live our lives is just long enough to eat and enjoy a wild strawberry.

If we follow the stories about the Big Bang that they now say launched the physical universe, and if we think how many billions of stars there are with no life, we wonder at the miracle of life on planet earth. In another billion years the energy may all dissipate, or another star might collide with our sun. So what. We have time today to pick a wild strawberry and enjoy it and give thanks.

Ever since Hiroshima, and now with 60,000 nukes on earth, we look down and see that tiger opening its jaws. Please hand me a strawberry!

God help us to see and to accept life as a divine gift, and to enjoy it today.

Share Simple Pleasures!

ONE OF THE NICE THINGS ABOUT GROWING OLDER is that we can SHARE as we enjoy the simple pleasures of life, like singing and playing and eating together.

SHARING is so important for us, because many would be staying in loneliness without some Caring Fellowship. We take this for granted too easily, but let's be thankful right now for our opportunities to help each other. With sharing, life can be heavenly but without it, life is hell.

Olive Schreiner once had a Dream about hell: She saw people gathered at a great banquet table which was laden with delicious food of all kinds. The people, however, were not eating and they looked very sad. Then she noticed each one had their arms bound in splints and they couldn't eat a single bite of the banquet before them. The dream suddenly was changed; she was in heaven. She saw people gathered at a great banquet table with elegant food, just as in hell. Then she noticed that all the people had their arms bound with splints, just as in hell. But these people were feasting and rejoicing, in happiness and love: THEY WERE FEEDING EACH OTHER!

Sharing there must be—every hour of every day—because no one is an island. All of us are bound together in the bundle of life. We are more keenly aware of it than younger people may be. And that is why it is worth celebrating.

God help us to keep our hearts and our eyes open to the needs of others around us, and of others around the world who are our brothers!

No More Deadlines!

ONE OF THE NICE THINGS ABOUT GROWING OLDER is that we don't have so many deadlines. As for me, the nicest thing about being retired is to forget the datebook most of the time. All of my professional life I was fighting deadlines. In college and graduate school it was exams and term papers. In my forty years as a pastor it was next Sunday's sermon or Tuesday night's Board agenda or Friday's bulletin announcements. I lived with my little datebook in my pocket and a big datebook at my church office and one in my study at home. And I always hoped that all three would match.

After retirement, life begins to return to a normal flow of seasons and events, with enough time to meet things as they come. It's a nice thing about growing older that we can begin to see life in the true perspective of eternity, instead of being slaves to the time clock and calendar.

Some older folks run the risk of boredom. But that's only if we have missed God's awakening call to each sparkling new day and the rhythm of the seasons when the Audubon Warblers come in October and leave for the mountains again in April.

We live by a daily schedule that helps us know what will happen next, although we can be flexible. For some (especially victims of Alzheimer's) the feeling of security in a regular schedule is important. But we don't have any deadlines in the usual sense, I'm glad to say.

God help us to live in the midst of time, accepting what comes that cannot be changed but changing what we can. And God help us to keep a window open on Eternity.

Discovering Courage

ONE OF THE NICE THINGS ABOUT GROWING OLDER is that we discover how much courage we really have.

I constantly admire those who live with serious disabilities: it means they have to summon great courage just to get from the bed to the wheelchair every morning. Others have disabilities that don't show so obviously, but still call for our best courage to face life each day.

My own experience of facing disability was not for myself, for I've been brazenly healthy all these 75 years. It was my son Jim, who had to drop out of college in his freshman year, and at the Menninger Clinic was diagnosed as epileptic. For 20 years, until his final accident, he lived on the brink every hour of every day, never knowing when the next seizure would knock him down. Though heavily medicated, he was one of the 40% whose seizures weren't fully controlled. Not able to drive a car, he rode his bike day and night. He made it a point to know every cop and every fireman, so if they ever had to pick him up—which they had to do sometimes—they wouldn't mistake him for a drunk or a junkie. He was generous to a fault, "loaning" money to wayfarers when he was living on a pittance. He's the only church member I've ever met who went hungry to keep up his church pledge. But now we're talking about courage—the risk it takes just to walk across the street when disability may tempt one to hold back and sit tight and be safe.

Every physical challenge has its heroes—people who cope, who will not give in or give up. Day by day they show us all what real courage is.

Life is indeed an adventure, every minute of every day. God help us to give honor and credit to those who need special courage just to survive from day to day. And may the rest of us keep humble and give thanks to God.

On Being Tough And Tender

ONE OF THE NICE THINGS ABOUT GROWING OLDER is that we can freely admit we are sentimentalists and romantics. We can show tender feelings with no embarrassment.

Many younger men nowadays feel the urge to act tough, macho, whether they really feel that way or not. The Rambo mentality is popular. Maybe it has roots going way back to the caveman. Maybe it's a cover-up for very insecure feelings, for many who cultivate the image.

Carl Jung, as I read him, seems to suggest that aggressive attitudes are "normal" for the human male, and the tender side of man's nature is repressed into what he calls the Anima, to be lifted up or rediscovered in the later years of life. I hope that most men are "normally" tender all along. I hope Jung is wrong in seeming to leave tenderness to the female of the species.

I surely agree with Jung, however, that in the second half of life, if men have previously repressed their tender feelings, such feelings can now blossom freely.

According to this dichotomy, women are always tender, accepting, self-effacing, even masochistic. If it's true, don't tell that to a "woman's libber"! The female of the species seems to have discovered aggressive, ego-affirming behavior (their supposedly buried "animus") without benefit of a Jungian analysis.

I hope I'm right that the norm for ALL of us is a healthy mixture of tough and tender feelings, assertiveness and sensitivity, held in balance. We all need some of each, I guess.

Now that we're retired, we don't "need" aggressiveness in business, or social climbing, or ego defense. Perhaps, with growing older, we can be truly mature and truly human. God help us to try!

We Don't Need Things

ONE OF THE NICE THINGS ABOUT GROWING OLDER is that we don't need things to be happy. They try hard almost 24 hours a day to sell us things. I really enjoy leafing through the ads and saying "I'm so glad we don't need anything in those ads!"

Our sales resistance gets stronger with each passing year. Pity the kids who think they have to buy the latest style, the newest fad — and pity their parents' credit cards! I have always warned young couples getting married that they will be deluged with high pressure ads, and to remember they don't need NOW all the things that their parents worked 25 years to get.

We live in a society now known for consumerism where expanding credit and huge debts are the norm — except for us old fogies who still pay for what we buy. Every year they say — and they hope — that THIS is going to be the big year for Christmas spending. The pressure is on in September, and it seems to increase all the way right up to Christmas Eve. Then they start on the year end specials and then the pre-inventory sales, and the going-out-of-business sales. Even then somebody gets rich and others don't. One rich retailer was overheard to say "I'm going to set up a store for my son so he can go out of business for himself." Now the catalogs are taking us over. That all began when roads were muddy and people couldn't get to town to shop. Now they bombard us all year. Send one order to one shop and it starts an avalanche. But sales resistance grows with each day's mail!

The simplification of life doesn't need to wait until we're old because all of us could get along with a shorter want-list. But when we're older, let us ENJOY the chance to simplify our desires, to streamline our wants, to give thanks that we have fewer THINGS TO KEEP TRACK OF.

God help us to see beyond things to the ultimate realities of Life.

Free To Believe

ONE OF THE NICE THINGS ABOUT GROWING OLDER is that we can be free to express our deepest beliefs and thoughts. What is there to lose? Why cover up our best cherished beliefs?

Says Dr. Paul Pruyser (in <u>Toward a Theology of Aging</u>, p. 116), "There is a clue to one satisfaction of aging in the penchant of exceptionally accomplished persons, particularly scientists, for writing in their advanced years about their beliefs, sharing with the public their personal credos. I am impressed by those works that reveal the writer's religious faith, which strike the reader as 'soft' in contrast to the hard-boiled rationality by which these men made their repute. Why does a man have to be old before he can speak up about his personal values, beliefs, or faith? I surmise that creative persons in their prime often...hide their deeper beliefs from their colleagues and the public so as not to disturb their image. As they grow older...they no longer hesitate to speak personally. They have wrestled themselves free from a very sophisticated form of thought control to which they first willingly submitted for the sake of their careers."

Aging, then, gives us new freedom for sharing our innermost thoughts. We no longer fear retaliation or mockery. In the second half of life, Jung contended, our problems and concerns are often of a religious nature. The process of "clarification" (Kunkel's term) or "Individuation" (Jung) brings to light the hidden depths within us and frees us to be our best selves. But it may take lots of interior work to face and overcome our hang-ups.

As a preacher for forty-five years, I often reflected on how I shared my deepest thoughts, week by week. In sermons (and prayers) I said more than I ever would in conversation. Yet I was always conscious of the question, "What will they think of me? Am I just a people-pleaser or am I, above all, true to God's Word?" For me at least, retirement has also brought a fuller sense of freedom. God help us all to be free to be our best!

In Spite Of

ONE OF THE NICE THINGS ABOUT GROWING OLDER is that, IN SPITE OF our aches and pains, IN SPITE OF our frustrating handicaps, we can still go on and live creatively and successfully.

We do many things IN SPITE OF many roadblocks, IN SPITE OF lots of skepticism. Someone said it this way:

"People are unreasonable, illogical, self-centered. Love them anyway. If you do good, people will accuse you of selfish, ulterior motives. Do good anyway. If you're successful, you'll win false friends and true enemies. Succeed anyway. The good you do today will be forgotten tomorrow. Do good anyway. Honesty and frankness make you vulnerable. Be honest and frank anyway. The biggest people with the biggest ideas can be shot down by the smallest people with the smallest minds. Think big anyway. People favor underdogs but follow only topdogs. Fight for the underdog anyway. What you spend years building may be destroyed overnight. Build anyway. People really need help, but may attack you if you help them. Help people anyway. Give the world the best you have and you'll get kicked in the teeth. Give the world the best you've got, anyway."

In other words, IN SPITE OF bits of cynicism that overtake us, IN SPITE OF all frustrations, we still keep trying to be part of the answer instead of part of the problem. Paul (in Rom. 8) put it in a noble phrase: "IN SPITE OF all these things, we are more than conquerors, through Christ who loves us. For I believe that neither life nor death, neither angels or demons, neither present or future, will ever be able to separate us from the love of God which is ours through Jesus Christ."

Whenever you feel depressed, take a fresh page in your notebook and head it IN SPITE OF; list all your gripes; then re-copy that verse from Romans. You'll feel better already!

A Little More Patience

ONE OF THE NICE THINGS ABOUT GROWING OLDER is that when we have to wait, we can do so with a little more patience and grace than we used to.

I used to be as bad as any husband – gritting my teeth if the wife and kids were still dressing when I was ready to leave. Of course if they had to wait a minute or five for me, that was different, for after all I was busy, wasn't I? Often tense, especially in a parsonage, was the Sunday Morning Syndrome, done to the tune of "Get Me to the Church on Time!"

John Burroughs must have been older or at least mellow when he wrote "Serene I fold my hands and wait...for lo, my own will come to me." In those days he wasn't waiting for his Social Security check, either. He must have had faith!

I'm still not very serene on the freeway when I try to leave a safe interval between cars and some young whipper- snapper cuts in front of me. Somebody said we all lose our Christianity when we sit behind a steering wheel! Elizabeth had me reading some doctor's advice column for those (like me) with borderline high blood pressure: discipline yourself to pick the longest line at the supermarket and stay in line. Stay in your lane on the freeway even if it's the slowest. I've tried it and it works – unless I'm in a hurry. But now that I'm older I'm not in a hurry quite as much of the time, and I'm glad.

I like to think of John Muir climbing to the top of a fir tree waiting patiently to watch a sunrise. I watch a spider by its web, waiting patiently for hours for some tiny insect to be in that corner of the garden. I remember how Thoreau patiently watched the changing drama of the seasons at Walden Pond.

I see God patiently watching as the glaciers carve out Yosemite. I think of God patiently nudging us on the long march of evolution. I know God is waiting for us stupid mortals to get a world government set up, and get nukes controlled, and get solar energy harnessed.

A New Kind Of Freedom

ONE OF THE NICE THINGS ABOUT GROWING OLDER is that we can begin to be a little bit detached from our possessions. There's an old saying, "You can't take it with you." That can be an ominous demand to face the fact that some day we will die and give up all possessions. But it can instead be a happy-go-lucky call to a new kind of freedom.

For too many people, their possessions own them, not vice versa. Many rich people, and many less than rich, are anxious 24 hours a day lest someone break in and steal their treasures. Such people also dread the doleful warning: "Thou fool, this night shall thy soul be required of thee; then whose shall all these things be?"

The only answer is to get detached from things now, and to see this as a joyous freeing of ourselves from bondage to things. In Hinduism and Buddhism this detachment from things and from desire for things is the very beginning of the path that leads to spiritual freedom. For many of the hippies and their descendants some variety of Neo-Hinduism involving radical simplification of life has likewise been a liberating experience.

Western individualism, with its worship of the ego and its cult of possessiveness, refuses to recognize that detachment is also the bottom rung of the ladder in Christianity. The first step in Jesus' code of happiness is, "Blessed are the poor in spirit." That means humility and teachableness but it certainly basically means giving up possessiveness.

All of us enjoy our souvenirs and trinkets and toys and that can be wholesome, provided they don't possess us. And beware if our "toys" are in the million dollar bracket!

When we grow older we can be carefree in a new and joyous sense. We can let others take over the worrying. We can recapture some of the zest and freedom of childhood, as Jesus suggested as a mark of entering the Kingdom. God help us to find the joy of such freedom.

Thanks With Every Breath

ONE OF THE NICE THINGS ABOUT GROWING OLDER is to be abundantly thankful for all the blessings we have received through the years. Of course we can be thankful at any age, but some younger folks think they have done it all by themselves, or worse yet that "the world owes them a living."

In Deuteronomy (8:11f) we are warned to "Take heed lest, when you have eaten and are full, and have built goodly houses and live in them, and your silver and gold is multiplied,... then your heart be puffed up with pride, and you forget the Lord your God.... Beware lest you say in your heart 'My power and my hand have gotten me this wealth.' You shall remember God, for it is the Lord God who gives you power to get wealth."

Giving thanks is not just a season of the year but a season of the heart, to remind us that we depend on God's gift of life and love in each moment of time. Frank Laubach used to suggest a Game With Minutes in which we would think of God thankfully for a few seconds in each minute of our waking day. Nobody could do that literally in a conscious act, but Brother Lawrence's Practice of the Presence of God suggests that such a spirit and attitude can underlie and undergird all our thoughts and actions.

To breathe a prayer of thanks brings God's many gifts to our conscious awareness. That is (or should be) the beginning of any real prayer, but it well may be the highest form of prayer also. For genuine thanks is also a measure of our receptiveness. God is always readier to give than we are to receive. The proud heart actually shuts God out, but the thankful heart that acknowledges our complete dependence on God enlarges our capacity to be channels of God's love. That means, of course, that we are thereby committed to pass on blessings to others. "The measure we give" said Jesus, "is the measure we receive." God help us to keep our lives open to be channels of blessing, to receive and to give.

Out Of The Jungle

ONE OF THE NICE THINGS ABOUT GROWING OLDER is that we can jump off the rat race. We no longer have to feel that the competition is catching up to us. We no longer have to keep polishing our image. We don't have to keep inventing new copy for our personal press agents. We can retire.

Vance Packard in <u>The Status Seekers</u> and White in <u>The Organization Man</u> (and many others) underlined some of the problems of men and women in the so-called creative years of life, given over to career-building and public achievement as well as just plain money-making. It's a jungle out there, they often say, by way of justifying jungle behavior in many cases. Aren't we glad to be out of that jungle!

One of Olive Schreiner's "Dreams" is about a jungle. It's one of her parables of hell. She dreamed she was in a great forest in which there were trails crisscrossing here and there. People were carefully threading their way along these trails. When they were gone, other people would rush out from behind the trees and dig a great pit right in the trail, and then cover it very carefully with branches and leaves. Then, hiding behind the trees again they would watch for some careless person who would walk along the trail and fall into the pit. Then they would rush out and cheer, because — in hell — they believed that when another person fell lower, they, by the same happening, raised higher. "The competition made us do it." Put someone else down and your stock goes up. Isn't that what gossip is all about too?

Now that the rat race is over for us, we can laugh about it. It's so nice to be retired. But on a deeper level we can also say (with John Donne) that when another is diminished, so am I, for "we are all involved in Mankind. Therefore send not to see for whom the bell tolls; it tolls for thee."

We don't have to prove anything except that we care for and accept each other, just as we know God accepts and cares for each one of us.

Enjoy The Sunset

ONE OF THE NICE THINGS ABOUT GROWING OLDER is having time to watch the sunset. In winter I can look out my study window to the sunset sky. Most of the year I sit on the sundeck by our little spa to watch the panorama.

Often I'm reading or writing or what my wife calls just shuffling papers, but the sunset gets the background of my attention and I hate to miss it.

Sometimes it's just gray California fog, but often there's a sunburst or a pageant of changing color. How richly God has blessed us, with a sunset each day of our lives. What if it was only once a year! The sunset is a window on Eternity and a pause that truly refreshes.

People say we ought to watch the sunrise and welcome the new day, but I've never been good at that. I have to have my coffee first, it seems.

At sunset I often notice the planes going by every half minute on their flight path to the L.A. airport. I think of the people heading homeward toward the sunset, and I pray they may find some peace of mind amid the bustle of the great and sprawling cities.

The house finches almost always join me at sunset. They perch on the wires that go along our creek bank and face toward the setting sun, singing their evening praises to God. I join, silently.

Sometimes I think about all the people in stores and offices and factories who hardly ever have time to watch a sunset. And I think of all the people, perhaps even more in number, who don't even care about sunsets. I feel sorry for them!

So ends another day, with the promise of another dawn, and an eternal dawning yet to come. Thanks be to God for each day and each sunset, and for the time to enjoy it all.

Exercise!

ONE OF THE NICE THINGS ABOUT GROWING OLDER is doing our morning exercises. Yesterday I was reading that many of us seniors just don't exercise enough.

One aerobics dance teacher has skillfully adapted her routines for those in wheelchairs or with other limitations. She tells us to stop if it hurts. But we all know we need to push ourselves to keep our muscles alive and to follow her lead to keep our minds alert too.

Those of us who are Strokies or Parkinsonians know that pushing muscles to the limit ("range of motion") sometimes does hurt and it takes work and will power. Perhaps we're like someone lost in a blizzard; we want to lie down and go to sleep, but if we do we're goners. To keep alive and alert is to keep struggling uphill. When we remember that, then there is fun in it too, for we can "rejoice like a strong man to run a race," as Psalm 19 puts it.

Speaking for myself, I've never jogged but I have often walked to the store or to church. I exercise at the end of a lawnmower or a garden shovel. I am amused and dismayed at those who feel the need to buy exercise equipment — and then pay someone else to mow their lawn.

Paul the Apostle was an exercise enthusiast apparently, and we know that he had to struggle to overcome some handicap of his own. He urged his friends at Philippi to follow his example in pressing on, like a runner seeking the prize, forgetting what is behind us and striving toward what is still ahead of us. He reminds us that the true goal is not just physical fitness, but the "upward call of God" to Christ-like living.

In the same vein Paul wrote to Timothy that physical fitness and discipline are good, but not nearly as important as spiritual fitness. We need both to live a full life.

God help us to keep alert and fit in body and mind and spirit, and to work at it every day.

Just For Today

ONE OF THE NICE THINGS ABOUT GROWING OLDER is that we can just live for today even if we forget the past and the future.

It used to be a sort of accusation to say someone was just living for today. It meant they were burning the candle at both ends and probably spending time and money recklessly and foolishly.

It all depends on what you mean by living for today. Jesus in the Sermon on the Mount says quite forcefully, "Take no thought for tomorrow, for tomorrow will take care of itself" OR "Don't worry about tomorrow; it will have enough worries of its own. Today's troubles are enough for today." I always want to add "Today's happiness also is enough to savor today."

There's no doubt Jesus meant us to live today to its fullest joy and highest possibility. Jesus said he came that we might have life more abundantly, now.

The philosophy of living one day at a time has been applied by Alcoholics Anonymous: Just for today I can be sober. I can be my best. I can live a new life. It works. Once I said it applies to all of us, Chocaholics and workaholics and everybody. "Christianity is like flying: If you stop, you drop!" One day at a time is all we have and it's all we need.

"Lord, for tomorrow and its needs I do not pray.
Keep me my God from stain of sin, just for today.
 Let me no wrong or idle word unthinking say.
Set Thou a seal upon my lips, just for today.
Let me both diligently work and duly pray.
O keep me in Thy loving care, just for today.
Let me in season Lord be grave, in season gay.
Let me be faithful to Thy grace.
And if today my tide of life should ebb away.
Grant me dear Lord Thy sacrament divine.
So for tomorrow and its needs I do not pray,
But keep me, guide and love me Lord, just for today."

The Sabbath Of The Soul

ONE OF THE NICE THINGS ABOUT GROWING OLDER is that we can enjoy THE SABBATH OF THE SOUL. This phrase is one of the loveliest images of happy retirement that I've heard. (Quoted by Robt. Katz in Hiltner Toward a <u>Theology of Aging</u> p. 148)

The Sabbath is a time of rest and thanksgiving and praise, after the work is done for now, and before a new adventure begins. Whether it's on Friday (Moslem), Saturday (Jewish and Adventist) or Sunday (Christian), the body and the mind both need "R and R" and the spirit needs worship time.

African travelers sometimes used to be grounded in the middle of nowhere, when their porters would declare a day off with the interesting comment, "We have to wait for our souls to catch up to our bodies." Our so-called civilization does not do well if we ignore this rhythm of the soul, or if on days off we turn to frenetic recreation that burns us out.

In retirement we can enjoy the Sabbath of the Soul every day—and we deserve it. As for myself, I confess to you I've been a workaholic, with an extreme case of "Protestant work ethic" that sometimes brought guilt feelings when I tried to loaf. My briefcase went along on almost every picnic or vacation (and still does).

But I'm learning to enjoy loafing so sometimes I can even sit back and watch the weeds grow in the garden. As I write these lines I'm sitting in the spa. The air is dry and 88 degrees. The solar-heated spa is 96. The birds are singing and the avocados are ripening in the tall tree overhead. Am I working or is this the Sabbath?

I remember Teviot in "Fiddler on the Roof," longing to be rich enough so he could sit in the Synagogue to discuss the Holy Book. Amazingly, one of the first things I did when I retired was to read the Bible through "from cover to cover." I had never done it before. It took a month. It was a beautiful Sabbath. God help us to grow in love and grace and truth each day of our new Sabbath!

Time To Smell A Rose

ONE OF THE NICE THINGS ABOUT GROWING OLDER is to take time to smell the flowers. Someone calls it a thirty second vacation, to pause and relax and enjoy a beautiful flower, and it's a good prescription for stress.

To smell a flower is also one more way to renew our kinship with Nature, and to give thanks to God for beauty and joy in life. The act of bowing down to smell a flower, and even more so to kneel and to weed and cultivate, is an act of humility. I was recently reminded that the word humility comes from humus which means earth. To be humble is to be earthy, to get off our high horse and to accept our relatedness to all of life.

In our little rose garden at home, we enjoy every color and each beautiful bloom, but we cultivate especially the old-fashioned fragrant varieties, like the Hadley and Mister Lincoln. There are so many others too, each with its special appeal.

In Southern California we are blessed with many tropical flowers, some of them with rich perfume and spectacular colors, designed to attract insects in the jungle. They attract people too!

Here we can have flowers all year, not all of them fragrant but all graceful and colorful and beautiful. Let us be thankful for them as truly gifts of God's love. And let us also be thankful for those who can share with others the lovely treasures of their gardens.

I suggested that pausing to notice the flowers keeps us in tune with Nature and with God. It does that and more—it keeps our senses keen and alert, and it ties us to the here and now of human experiencing. This helps us to live this present moment to the fullest and thereby to open anew our windows to Eternity.

Using Burnt Stones

ONE OF THE NICEST THINGS ABOUT GROWING OLDER is the realization that God can use us, just as we are, in the recycling and re-creation of life. Nehemiah led the Jews returning from Babylon in rebuilding the city of Jerusalem. It's an exciting bit of history that the Persian King sent Nehemiah with supplies and funds to rebuild the city destroyed at the time of the exile. But there were problems, and there were those who tried to block the rebuilding. Sanballat was a local politician whose power would be lost if Nehemiah succeeded, so he picketed the project and shouted: "Who is this who brags about rebuilding this old city? And he would use burned stones at that!"

Second hand building blocks were a source of derision, and they often are today. Everything has to be new. Clear away the rubble and start from scratch. It costs more to repair the old building than to begin from zero.

But that isn't always the case. At the hardware supermarket used bricks cost more than new bricks, because there's a charm that old things have. Antiques are often better made than the contemporary models. Our son has rebuilt the engine and transmission on an older car because the new cars are worse than old ones. In Europe, cathedrals damaged in war were sometimes patiently rebuilt with the same stones.

When I visited Sancta Sophia in Instanbul I was amazed to hear that this exquisite sanctuary has in it columns stones from a dozen or more ancient temples of the Near East. At that time it was the rule that pillars and columns would be recycled. And in the walls of ancient cities it was inevitable because the "burned stones" were there in piles, waiting to be recycled! Nehemiah was right. God can use burned stones. God can recycle old ideas and old people in the renewal of the world. Employers are learning that older workers have important experience, valuable skills, less sick leave and more consistent work records than many younger workers. Let's not let Sanballat make fun of us! God can and does use "burnt stones" from the old Jerusalem to build the New Jerusalem!

Look more carefully at the Universe and see how recycling goes on all the time. The water cycle keeps rivers flowing and nourishes life. The carbon cycle brings renewal through all life forms. Oxygen recycles from plants to air to animal life and back again. Cells in our bodies die and are reborn again. Call it the miracle of death and resurrection, and thank God always.

I Don't Know

ONE OF THE NICE THINGS ABOUT GROWING OLDER is that we don't have to have opinions on all subjects. We can say I DON'T KNOW without any embarrassment!

When I was a college kid I thought I had all the answers or at least I'd find them soon. But now that I'm 75 I've decided I don't have to know everything. Sometimes I can just enjoy!

I remember when my Ph.D. son tried to teach me all about how a computer works, and just how nuclear fusion happens. And my microbiologist daughter explained how DNA works or how carcinogens take over cells. I listened and I partly got the story, but I admit it was over my head. I don't have to know the details to appreciate the wonders of this world.

At least 20 years ago I gave up trying to understand international monetary controls (or the lack of them). I don't understand it. But what I DO know is enough to scare me: how bad debts to U.S. banks are passed on to US in the form of inflation.

Mark Twain, as a biblical commentator (!) said that the parts of the New Testament that bothered him were not those he DIDN'T understand but those he DID understand! It may have been Mark Twain who also added: I know enough to do a good deal better than I usually do.

Thomas A. Kempis in his quaint words showed us proper humility: "The greater thy knowledge, the more severely shalt thou be judged. Therefore be not puffed up by any skill or knowledge that thou hast, but rather fear concerning the knowledge which is given thee. Know also that there are many more things which thou knowest not. BE NOT HIGH-MINDED, but rather confess thine ignorance."

God help us to be humble and to keep learning!

New Possibilities

ONE OF THE NICE THINGS ABOUT GROWING OLDER is that we have a better chance of glimpsing the possibilities of life. There are some who see older age as only a matter of shrinking possibilities, but it is not so. In younger years we were tied down with the specific responsibilities of our job and raising our families. With our noses to the grindstone we had little time to see life in its larger perspectives.

Now that we are retired, we can let our imagination roam in a new creative sense. Matthew Fox in Original Blessing (p.235), suggests that the imagination of possibilities and the awakening of possibilities is part of the very process of salvation for people who have felt locked in and put down.

I'm not a fan of Robert Schuler, but I do enthusiastically support his technique of "Possibility Thinking." Too often we have let ourselves be locked in by the past, by what others think of us, by stereotypes, by little habits of thinking. God constantly seeks to liberate us from our past, to renew our minds from within, to kindle New Life within us.

I once helped to start a "HOT-LINE" telephone counseling service, and I was on call any time of the day or night, and especially when no other volunteer wanted to take the calls! I remember how often I used to listen to someone whose life seemed to be locked into a dilemma with no way out. Sometimes it seemed all the person needed was money. But often it was merely the imagination to see some third or fourth way out of the situation. I tried hard and often I succeeded in suggesting some other ways to explore, with courage and with faith. I asked them to call me again and sometimes they did, to report a new lease on life.

Way back in the thirties I wrote an article called THIRD ALTERNATIVES to try to explode the stupid myth that dominates international and intergroup relations that either I WIN or YOU WIN. I'm up and you're under my heel or vice-versa and there is no alternative. But there always is at least one alternative—the creative resolution of differences in which everyone comes out a winner. Are you going to be a doormat and let them walk all over you? OR are you going to be a Rambo Bully and walk all over them? Is there no alternative? Just how stupid can we be—of course there are other possibilities. It takes a little imagination and a little creativity and then something really new could happen.

The world is waiting for some old folks like you and me to think and dream and imagine and create new alternatives before this old world goes down to destruction. God help us to do it, in time!

Love God In Silence

ONE OF THE NICE THINGS ABOUT GROWING OLDER is that we can accept God's love without having to talk about it. In the silence of our hearts, we know more about God than we dare to say out loud. Maybe that's why we like to sing the old time hymns, because they voice something of what we feel inside, but someone else gives us words to feel our faith affirmation. The theological details are less important than the feeling of faith that is in us.

Meister Eckhart warns us to "be silent and do not flap your gums about God!" (quoted by M. Fox in BREAKTHROUGH). God is the unknowable and unnameable, always beyond and above any description we can give with mere words. There is a time to be silent.

I plead guilty, however, to having spent much of my life in trying to teach people about the love of God in reasonable terms. I believe we can and must have a faith that fits the best we know of science and art and history, – yet always goes beyond them. Faith can be understandable as well as remaining a mystery.

One lad is said to have defined faith as "believing what you know ain't so." Faith is believing what you can't prove by science or by logic – but that merely describes the limits of scientific and logical method. Faith always goes beyond.

Meister Eckhart would have to admit that he spent his life in using words, often paradoxical words, to express what is beyond words. Some of his paradoxes were so startling they got him in trouble.

God help us to be like children, open to accepting God's love even though we can never "explain" God. But let's not be afraid to keep asking questions and seeking answers.

A Future For The World

ONE OF THE NICE THINGS ABOUT GROWING OLDER is that we can imagine a real future for the world because we have lived through so many crises in the past.

I don't minimize the nuclear peril and the apocalyptic threat to all life on planet earth. I've talked about that and I'll keep on! But I do say that old age can give us a perspective and a kind of toughness that is called maturity, or even serenity, or perhaps Faith.

I recall the story of a young missionary who had just arrived in the field, amidst fear and tension. With typical youthful arrogance he declared, "I guess I arrived just in the nick of time." The seasoned veteran replied: "Well, I've been here for 30 years and it's been getting nicker all the time."

I've been reading (and reviewing) a book about the "nuclear winter" that might follow a full scale nuclear war. It's sobering and even frightening. The only defense is peace. It's hard to keep a perspective with that threat in the foreground.

The great philosopher Emerson finished a lecture and a wild-eyed young man came up and shouted, "How can you be so calm when the world is coming to an end?" "Well," Emerson is said to have replied, "I guess we'll learn to get along without it."

That's a level of serenity I can't claim for myself. But I do know that as I have grown older I can see crises come and go and still keep faith in a future for mankind.

God help us to create that future by our attitudes and our prayers and our actions.

47

We Have Time Today

ONE OF THE NICE THINGS ABOUT GROWING OLDER is that we don't have to be slaves of the alarm clock any more. We can live in tune with the rhythm of days and nights, getting up a little earlier in summer and sleeping over on winter mornings.

I used to be a night owl and sometimes study till 1 or 2 in the morning. It seemed important then, to finish that book or that writing. But I had to depend on the alarm the next morning!

In one sense we oldsters are running out of time, but in another sense we have time to do what is important or just what we want to do. We have time every morning.

A Spanish poet named Antonio Machado said that the most important thing Jesus said was: "WAKE UP!" That doesn't mean just getting up without an alarm clock, though. It means waking up to God in our lives: coming alive to God's Kingdom now. It means rediscovering that God's Love is the most real thing in the Universe and all else is secondary and derived. We try to wake up to that Reality every morning.

Meister Eckhart preached a sermon on the text in Luke 7: "YOUNG MAN, I TELL YOU TO GET UP!" This wasn't just getting up in the morning but rising from death, finding a new life, and Jesus could do it. Rediscovering God's infinite power and love means rising to a new level of consciousness, and Jesus says we can all do it.

As we grow older we have fewer things to distract us from this important agenda of life. God help us to work at it today.

From the Ancient East comes this awakener:

> LISTEN TO THE SALUTATION OF THE DAWN.
> Look to this day, for it is life, the very
>   Life of life.
> In its brief course lie all the verity and reality of your existence, —
>   The bliss of grow,
>   The splendor of beauty,
>   The glory of action.
> For yesterday is but a dream,
>   and tomorrow is only a vision, —
> But today well lived, makes every yesterday
>   a dream of happiness,
>   And every tomorrow a vision of hope.
> Look well, therefore, to this day.

The Great Adventure

ONE OF THE NICE THINGS ABOUT GROWING OLDER is that we can make friends with Death, and understand him not as our enemy but as our friend.

Many younger people just try to repress any thoughts about death, and some say that's why they keep their stereos turned up so loud and why they rush around so fast. Or are they trying to get away from having to face and accept themselves?

Someone has written a book about the last third of life and he seems to say that coming to grips with our own death is a top priority for this last third of life. It seems to me that living fully each day and accepting ourselves fully is the best way to realize that life and death belong naturally together as part of God's loving plan for each one of us. My experience with older people is that most of us fear pain and helplessness more than we fear death, and some day we will welcome death as a friend. Someone expressed it this way:

"HERE, surrounded by my mother's womb, I am safe and content.
Nowhere, I tell myself, could life be better than here.
How sad that some day I must leave this warm engulfment,
    this nearness of all that I hold dear.
How sad that I must some day be born!
And then comes that great adventure — Birth!

"Strange I did not know the joys that it would bring.
Strange I did not know they would be deeper and greater
    than any I had known before.
    But there in the dark enshrouding womb I could not envision a richer life.
I could not know the joy of birdsong on May mornings,
    of frost that bejewels even ragged weeds,
    of stream and flower and autumn's bright trembling leaf.
I could not know the abiding joy of friendship,
    the ever deepening joy that links wife to husband, and to child...
I could not know the joy of great music, and haunting little tunes,
    and great books, and bits of verse...
I could not know the joy of growth that rides triumphant
    even in the wake of failure and loss."

Now, surrounded by my earthly life, I'm safe and content. Nowhere, I tell myself, would life be better than here.

"How sad that I must someday leave this sweet engulfment,
    this nearness of all I hold dear.
How sad that some day I must die.

Then suddenly I remember.

"Long years ago I was not enraptured with being born.
    I could not envision a richer life.
Once again it is the same. Once again the enshrouding womb of the present
    keeps me from glimpsing the richer life to come.

Now I understand.

"O Death,
You, too, are a great adventure,
Planned in the loving heart of God,
    for the joy of all who lie within the circle of his care.

O Death, whate'er your hour of coming, I welcome You!"

Today Is A Holiday

ONE OF THE NICE THINGS ABOUT GROWING OLDER is that we can make every day a holiday! A holiday seems to mean just loafing or watching a football game on TV, but when we're retired, maybe we have to come back to the original meaning of the word: a holiday is a holy day. And that's what everyday really is.

By "the Holidays" we usually mean Thanksgiving and Christmas (or Hanukkah) and New Year's all rolled into one great festive time. Greeting card people begin getting ready for the holidays back in January or February. But we all do it too. We put away the Christmas ornaments planning to use them again next Christmas. Perhaps we say, well, next year we'll do it differently. Kids begin thinking by summertime what they're going to get next Christmas, and adults more and more begin their shopping in the fall or summer.

The point is, it all adds up to a lot of big expectations, lots of hopes and fears too. For many people the holidays are the high point of the year. Then afterward there's a big let-down. No more lights and decor. No more big parties or family gatherings to look forward to. After the holidays there are always some deaths and even some suicides. People have held out, and then they give up.

There's another reason for unhappiness and even suicide during holiday time. We assume that everyone else is happy celebrating and we are lonely and despair sets in. If the truth were fully known, many people are unhappy in the midst of family gatherings, for old jealousies dating way back to childhood may resurface, and new jealousies and resentments and guilt feelings emerge during what should be the happiest days.

Let's get back to the now, today. Today may not be a holiday but it is a holy day: a day to celebrate life, to remember that there are new joys and possibilities open to us.

> Awake, my soul, stretch every nerve,
>   and press with vigor on.
> A heavenly race demands thy zeal,
>   and an immortal crown.
>
> A crowd of witness around
>   hold thee in full survey.
> Forget the steps already trod,
>   and onward urge thy way.
>
> Tis God's all-animating Voice
>   that calls thee from on high.
> Tis God's own hand presents the prize
>   to thine uplifted eye.

Have I Not A Life To Give?

ONE OF THE NICE THINGS ABOUT GROWING OLDER is that we do have our life in our hands now—to use and spend and give.

Even oldsters like us can make a difference. The Grey Panthers tell us we have power at the polls, and that older people are more likely to vote than younger ones, strange as it seems. There is something each one of us can do—or we wouldn't be here!

I want to share with you a very dramatic story to show what I mean by having our life in our hands, to use and to give. This true story was told by Mabel Shaw (in God's Candlelights) who was a missionary in Africa.

"One clear evening I went down to the leper camp at the end of our village. There were very few of them there. It was not a pleasant place....

"I listened to all their troubles; then we talked of other things, and soon we were laughing over some absurd story. They told me a lion had been about, and showed me the spoor by a little stream. That opened another topic of conversation. At last I rose to go. I gave a last word and greeting, promised I'd remember all their needs, and was just about to mount my bicycle, when out of one of the little houses came the old leper head-man. He held a spear between the stumps that once were hands, and he went hobbling along the path in front of me. I called to him, and he stopped and looked around. 'Where are you going?' 'I am going to escort you to the village; you can't go alone with lions about.' I smiled at him. 'But on my bicycle I'll be there in a minute.'

"He would not have it. It was not fitting for me to go alone. I looked at him, a feeble old man, handless, feet half-eaten, his whole body covered with marks of disease and his face most pitiful. I said to him, half jokingly, and with a smile, 'Now what could you do if a lion came?' He drew himself up, and with quiet dignity he said, 'Have I not a life to give?'

"I was silent, seeing a Cross. I followed him to the village, thanked him and came home, having met with God face to face...."

Yes, we do have our life to give, to live. We can still be part of the answer instead of part of the problem, in this old world. God help us to remember that the world is still in God's hands, and that we are too. Let's live that way today.

When Dreams Come True

ONE OF THE NICE THINGS ABOUT GROWING OLDER is that we can dream, and help at least some of our dreams to come true.

I don't mean nightmares or night dreams. This time I mean DAY DREAMS, and some of them point toward making this old world a better place.

Architects and city planners are professional dreamers. When they have a building or a civic center visualized, and when the blueprints are done, the project seems more than half complete. And when the foundations are laid and the structure begins to appear above ground, the job is almost accomplished.

They say the way to hell is paved with good intentions, and that of course warns us that we have to back up our fine words with good deeds. But I say to you that the way to heaven is also paved with good intentions! Unless we dream it, envision it, intend it, it probably can never happen.

In the Bible it says, "Your old men shall dream dreams and your young men shall see visions" and we assume that youth is a time for visions. But the old men and their dreams are mentioned first by the prophet, and we'll update him to include the ladies also!

One dream I had years ago was to see freeways built on the second story level, with factories and stores beneath them facing on the streets. In a few places the space under freeways is used to park cars, but in most cities that's about all.

Our dreams of a world at peace are lots more important. World problems are complex, but the answers are out there — or in here! We have to begin with dreams and prayers and good intentions, and then lots of hard work.

Someone said it well: STAND UP AND BECOME YOUR PRAYER! God help us to do it, today.

Give and Receive Blessing

ONE OF THE NICE THINGS ABOUT GROWING OLDER is that we can give blessings and receive blessings with an open and thankful heart.

Nowadays to say a blessing seems to be confined to a prayer and thanks before a meal. This is important and we should never forget it, even when we are in a place where the blessing is silent and even when there is noise around us. It's never too noisy for us to give thanks to God in our inmost hearts. Indeed, some say we would ideally breathe a prayer of thanks to God with every mouthful of food, remembering that life itself is a gift of God, and also remembering the millions who do not have the abundance of food that we have.

But in ancient Israel the blessing was a formal and very solemn occasion when an old man, foreseeing his own death, would gather his children and grandchildren about him and speak special words of blessing to each one and at the same time announce his inheritance to each. It was the equivalent of writing a will, only much more personal.

Another kind of blessing is the benediction, for the Latin word really means blessing. We do this at the end of worship and sometimes when loved ones are parting from each other.

Jesus spoke the famous blessings that we now call the Beatitudes. He said, "Blessed are you." I understand that the word he used had that personal meaning even though we now phrase it, "Blessed are the poor in spirit." In Luke it reads, "Blessed are you poor, for yours is the Kingdom of Heaven."

When the clerk in the bank or grocery store says to me, "Have a good day," I hear that as a blessing and I try to bless silently in return. Like any phrase it can become trite and meaningless. But we can make it alive and beautiful by what it means inside the words.

God bless us and make of our lives a blessing to others.

Renewed From Within

ONE OF THE NICE THINGS ABOUT GROWING OLDER is that "although our outer nature is wasting away our inner nature is being renewed every day." Those were Paul's words in II Corinthians 4:16.

A book I just read about a "practical theology of aging" seems to make that sound like a dualism of body and spirit, but it isn't at all. It could be what is called compensation: for instance, a blind person develops a keener sense of hearing and of touch. One who loses the use of legs may develop stronger shoulder muscles. One who loses the use of a right arm may learn to eat and write and paint left-handed.

Although body, mind and spirit are one unity, just as sight and hearing are part of a unity, there is a law of compensation at work.

I remember back through many thousands of pastoral visits to people who were chronically or terminally ill, how often I left such a visit strengthened and inspired by the spirit of the person shining through a broken body. One dear 94-year-old who had not been able to attend even one worship service during my years as a pastor, always greeted me with the question, "Well, how goes the Work?" She was always genuinely interested in my detailed reply, and she was in spirit and in truth an active partner in it.

One 72-year-old lady was so afflicted with arthritis that she could not even lift her fork to her mouth, but her 92-year-old mother took care of her. (They finally died within 5 days of each other.) But this amazing lady loved to quote poetry. We discussed literature and art, and invariably I went from her bedside refreshed and uplifted in spirit, looking forward to our next visit.

Not all sick people are saints. Not all well people are saints. But we CAN be renewed day by day, from within. God help us to be renewed by the power of the Spirit, today.

What We Have Left

ONE OF THE NICE THINGS ABOUT GROWING OLDER is that we can be thankful not for what we've lost but for what we have left! Someone said that growing old isn't so bad when you consider the alternatives.

Harold Russell lost both hands in the war, and he uses hooks instead of hands. In an interview he said, "It's not what you lost in life that counts, it's what you do with what you have left."

Katharine Hepburn at age 75, challenging us to keep vital, refers to these great examples:

"Roosevelt had infantile paralysis. It didn't keep him down. Nothing could. Only death. He worked with what was left him; his head, his humor, his heart. And it made him a much richer and more generous creature. He'd had an experience very few have. It made him sensitive to the desperation of man. He had a project.

"Helen Keller: deaf, blind. She pursued life. She had a project. She made new senses.

"Mother Teresa: she is unique. No self problems; she lives entirely for others.

"George Bernard Shaw: he worked and worked and worked. He said he only hoped that when he died he would be all used up."

No excuses! Keep trying! Believe in yourself and your own vitality. Keep on with the pursuit of life, of pleasure, of excitement, of a new adventure. That's the message Kate repeats and she lives by it:

"We're surrounded by opportunities, aren't we? Isn't it exciting? Little opportunities and big ones.... How can we make life better? We may not find perfection but we can try. That's the pursuit of life itself, isn't it?"

God help us to make the best of what we have left and use our lives to capacity!

The Past Lives In Us

ONE OF THE NICE THINGS ABOUT GROWING OLDER is to remember vividly people and events of the past. And these cannot be taken away from us even if we forget the details. We literally tie the past and the future together: we make history within our own being.

Every time I drive through Oakland on the MacArthur Freeway I pass right UNDER where my folks lived for over 50 years. Soon after my mother died, the bulldozers arrived. The State had bought the house months before. Attic and basement were cleared of relics and keepsakes from all branches of the family, because those two people and their house had been symbols of steadfastness and permanence and trust, spanning three generations. Rare botanical specimens had been donated to several arboretums from that venerable garden. The bulldozers took care of the rest. But when I drive west in the fast lane of the freeway, I go through it all again!

In my memory I still see 40 California quail sitting on the wooden fence, when I was young and the house was on the edge of the city. I can still hear the hermit trush singing in the plum tree as he did every wintertime. I see 30 relatives gathering from far and near to sit down to Thanksgiving dinner and then sleep in every room or a tent on the lawn. I see my father, during the Great Depression winter evenings, bending over his accounts receivable book and wondering if he can collect enough to feed us all.

The freeway was of course progress and the old Victorian house is gone, but our grandchildren live on with their priceless heritage of faith and steadfastness. They will never see the house except in a few crinkled snapshots. They will never see the depression ledgerbook, although one granddaughter has preserved parts of it. But the stuff of pioneers and pilgrims is marching in their lives and ours, and that keeps us going today and tomorrow.

God help us to be true to those who have gone before us!

The Curtain-Call

ONE OF THE NICE THINGS ABOUT GROWING OLDER is to look forward with no fear or hesitation to our final curtain-call.

God put us on the stage of life, at first with shaky steps and faltering voices. We remember those who brought us up with patience and love, those who shared with us their wisdom and courage, those who coached us for our role in life's drama. We thank you Lord, for those we remember, and others long forgotten or never known by name, who helped to form the character we have become through the years. We give thanks for times when we began to forget who we really were and then you sent someone to remind us and to prompt us. When we sat in the wings, downcast and discouraged, we are grateful that someone stood us up and pushed us back on stage with a pat on the back or even a kick in the proper place.

So we are "on stage" for a few brief years, and it's an exciting way of thinking about our lives as a whole. It's rather interesting to note that the Sunday Church service has sometimes been compared to a show — by critics of the Church of course. Actually some TV evangelists have become showmen and actors to such an extent that it's confusing if not downright nauseating to many of the "audience."

Soren Kierkegaard, the somber Dane of another century, warned us that indeed the Church is a theater, but very different from what we usually imagine: The preacher, he says, is not on stage but is merely the one in the prompter's box; all of us, the people, are the ones on stage; and GOD IS THE AUDIENCE. Think about it!

When our final curtain-call has come, we hope and pray that The Audience will be ready to say: "Well done, good and faithful servant! Enter into the Joy of the Lord."

Happy Birthday To You

ONE OF THE NICE THINGS ABOUT GROWING OLDER is that we can celebrate our birthdays with no fears or regrets, and with no need to conceal our age. In fact, we can begin to be proud of our age. When we were 49 we probably joked about our 39th birthday. Some still do.

Forty used to be the cut-off point, the magic dividing line. Then someone wrote, and millions read, that "Life Begins at Forty." Lots of folks still have a compulsion to conceal their age. Now that we are older we can even brag a little.

My mother always concealed her age, and as I grew up I realized it was probably because she was nine years older than my father. In those days she apparently felt that a wife should certainly be of equal or younger age than her husband. But as I grew up, I vowed that I would be open and frank about my birthdays.

The only problem I had was in my first parish out of seminary, when some of the good (older) folks thought I was just a college kid and not quite their image of a "Reverend." The first funeral I ever had was in the family of an 8-year-old girl, and I talked with her a good deal, telling her among other things that I went by the nickname of Wim. Next Sunday morning she breezed into the Church lobby and in the shocked hearing of my sedate elders loudly shouted, "Hi, Wim!"

I find that my kids in their forties are more "afraid" of their next birthday than I am at 75. I already know that I'm older! We all know that the mid-life crisis has many aspects, but that an important ingredient is coming to grips with our own finiteness. It may take us 10 or 20 years to get over that hurdle, and some never do. But one of the very nice things about growing older is to put that hurdle behind us and celebrate birthdays with no regrets.

When Edwin Markham reached 80 he wrote and published Eighty Songs at Eighty. I read all of them once, when I was around 60. The main thing I remember now was his hearty challenge to the years that lie ahead: "Come on, I am ready for you!"

God help us to be ready to celebrate our next birthdays — and many more to come.

Spending Life To Find Life

ONE OF THE NICE THINGS ABOUT GROWING OLDER is to give to others our "last full measure of devotion" and to know the eternal satisfaction this brings. In our so-called declining years we can more easily discover the truth that "whoever spends (lays down) his life will indeed find Life."

The famous phrase from Lincoln's "Gettysburg Address" of course refers to the men who spent their lives on the field of battle, and their sacrifice is to be honored. Many others who give their lives in heroic although humble service to the common good also deserve honors. The "last full measure of devotion" means living for others not just "dying for them."

In other words we are not just talking about epitaphs and obituaries, but we are talking about honoring people for public or private self-giving service for others. And now we are saying that the satisfaction it brings is not some ephemeral wisp but an actual new lease on life. We can begin to document the old saying that virtue is its own reward. Goodness does pay dividends. Self-giving love does give power back to the giver in return.

Margaret Runbeck (in The Great Answer) tells the true story of Jewish refugees fleeing from the Nazis into the south of France and then over the Pyrenees to freedom in Spain. It was a perilous climb on foot, and this time through winter snow, but they had already risked their lives to get there. By secret signals they were made known to the young leader, but to his dismay at the last moment came a young woman with a babe. And so they set out, well before dawn, people of all ages. Soon the leader was carrying the babe, for the younger mother was frail from persecutions. As they struggled up through rocks and snow, one of the oldest men fell and would not move, telling the others to go and let him die in peace. The young leader stood over him: "Your life is gone, but with your last breath before you die, carry this child who must go on to freedom." The old man took the child and arose and his strength returned. In giving his life for another, life was given back to him in return.

Sail Forth, O Soul

ONE OF THE NICE THINGS ABOUT GROWING OLDER is to be able to launch out into the deeps of the Spirit with no fear or hesitation. I'm not suggesting a Shirley Maclaine trip, but just an open and expectant spirit, not ruling out the mysteries and the miracles that surround us.

God calls us to new adventures. The greatest unexplored frontier is inside the human brain! We are only beginning to learn the secrets of nerve impulse transmission, and how the memory really works (or does not work), and how knowledge is related to wisdom and to meanings and values. And the exciting thing is that each one of us has a laboratory and a think tank right where we are now!

My grandfather's last sermon in Kohala, Hawaii (he died there on a Sunday afternoon in 1893, serving as a Congregational Missionary) was based on the text "Launch out into the deep." Jesus, as recorded in Luke 5, was chiding his fishermen disciples for their quick discouragement when they failed to make a catch. When they followed his advice and launched out into deeper waters they found abundant and unexpected blessing.

Let's remember some of our own brightest moments in past years, when adventurous faith was rewarded with a great "catch" beyond our expectations. Perhaps we had been saying, "I probably can't do it" or "I tried once and didn't succeed" or "There are too many strikes against me" or "Someone else will probably get there first." It's time to launch out with faith. To many a hesitant person looking for a job and seeing not too many openings beckoning, I have said, "You don't need too many openings — just one!" Several times I've had to say that to myself too.

Always God's challenge to new adventure and new life is before us.

Walt Whitman voiced the challenge eloquently in "Passage to India."

> Sail forth, O soul,
> Steer for the deep waters only:
> Reckless, O soul, exploring,
> For we are bound where mariner has not yet dared to go!
> O daring joy, but safe —
> Are they not all the seas of God?
> O my brave soul, O farther, farther sail!

Enjoying Old Clothes

ONE OF THE NICE THINGS ABOUT GROWING OLDER is that we don't really have to follow the latest style in clothes. The style-conscious youngsters are probably going to call us "old fogies" anyway, so we may as well make the best of it and enjoy our old clothes. Besides, if we do attempt the latest fad they'll say we're trying to act like kids.

I have six suits in the closet and I hardly ever wear them nowadays. But when I want to dress up, I have my choice. The legs are probably too wide or too narrow and the lapels are also. Then there are the skirts you ladies keep in your closets: some too long and some too short and some too medium. But in a few years they'll be in style again!

We in turn can joke a bit about the latest kid's styles. Remember when they began the loose floppy look and we called it "vintage Goodwill?" For 50¢ at the thrift shop you could probably get a close approximation to what the kids pay $40 for. Every six months the ad men come up with some new twist, but it usually looks about the same to us oldsters. When I wear some favorite old tie (when I wear one) they probably say it's too wide or too narrow. And I say so what.

When my old garden jeans look worn or faded or patched, they are. Now the kids pay big prices to have them look faded or even patched when they're brand new. The brand label, of course, accounts for much of the price. Somebody has to pay for the advertising campaigns.

I don't ski but I have a great ski parka that I wear in the mountains or on extra cold winter mornings (we have a few even here in California). It's nearly 40 years old and the nylon hasn't faded and the zipper works perfectly. Since then they invented the zippers that self-destruct within two years to make you buy new clothes. That must be progress in this era they call consumerism. But I still like some of my old clothes best, and I'll bet you do too!

Laughing At Limitations

ONE OF THE NICE THINGS ABOUT GROWING OLDER is that we can learn to laugh at our limitations. "The old gray mare she ain't what she used to be." We probably learn that we have to move a little slower with a few creaky joints, but that doesn't stop us. We may take a little longer to get some things done, but we have the time!

Then there's our bi-focals or tri-focals that teach us to walk a bit more carefully and perhaps to step a little higher over the curb. We may have a hearing aid to compel us to keep more alert as to the direction and quality of the sounds around us. Perhaps we can even tune out some of the static and the noise-overkill that invades our lives these days.

From every direction we are getting conflicting advice on what to eat and what not to eat. There has been a battle going on among the experts (and I'm sure it isn't over yet) as to whether cholesterol is a serious danger to be avoided at all costs, or like many things to use carefully and in moderation. Only a few days ago I heard some health "expert" warning us that oleo margarine may be just as "bad" for us as butter was said to be. Who can we believe? And just who is paying these experts?

Lots of the latest health advice is just what we always knew: a balanced diet with plenty of fruits and vegetables, and chew it lots and never be under any stress at mealtime. For people in a rush and on the go and addicted to fast foods, this sounds pretty unrealistic. But for us elders it can make life longer as well as more enjoyable.

Of course our intentions are often better than our performance. We eat now, and regret later. My dad used to admit,"I can resist anything but temptation!"

Bill Cosby tells us that when he was 15 he used to chomp down jalapeno peppers in front of the girls and they'd laugh and say, "Man, you're crazy!" and that was a compliment. When he was fifty (that was only a couple of years ago) he ate one jalapeno pepper in front of his wife and she said, "Man, you're crazy!" and she meant it. And he admitted that his tummy burned all night like the fires of Atlanta. Now, when Bill Cosby gets to be 75, he probably won't even want to try to chomp down a jalapeno pepper!

Diminishments are many and various and inevitable in elderhood. We can cry or we can laugh. But we can laugh only if we see beyond them and through them to those things that endure.

A Gateway Opens

ONE OF THE NICE THINGS ABOUT GROWING OLDER is to look back on our lives and realize, at critical points perhaps, that God has guided us and blessed us beyond our knowing or our deserving. We usually call it Providence.

To the people of Israel God said repeatedly through the Prophets: I have lifted you up and blessed you not because you deserve it, but in order that My Righteousness may be known among all peoples. Looking back in later years they realized that they were guided and blessed in strange and wonderful ways.

Remembering my own pilgrimage, there were times when the future seemed like a blank wall. Where was the next step to be? And then, when all doors seemed to be closing, a new gateway opened.

And here is a parable to remember. From my study window in Grand Junction, I could and did look out toward the Colorado National Monument with its majestic red cliffs and canyons and to the south of it the expanse of Pinyon Mesa. There were many canyons leading from among the great cliffs to the Grand Valley below. One of them was called No Thorofare Canyon because, tracing up the creek-bed through ancient granite one came at last to a vast amphitheater with vertical red rock walls. What looked like an escape route became No Thorofare! (Actually my sons and I found by adventurous exploring that the Indians who lived there until about 900 A.D. had built one tiny trail up over the rim rock.)

Farther south on the Mesa, the notch also visible from my study window, was a similar canyon leading up from the valley through huge boulders and finally into a great amphitheater. But lo and behold, it became a broad green meadow leading through to another canyon descending to the west. Gateway Canyon it is called, and a paved highway leads through it to the uranium country beyond!

Two canyons there are on Pinyon Mesa, and they look alike from the valley below. One is No Thorofare, but the other is a Gateway to new promise and new life. May God help us at every moment of frustration and despair, to keep exploring until we find the Gateway that opens on a new vista of hope and joy.

All Life Is One

ONE OF THE NICE THINGS ABOUT GROWING OLDER is realizing anew the oneness of all life, which can come with some of the mellow feelings and the liberating visions of elderhood. Once we have escaped from the proverbial rat race and retired from the mad scramble for money and power, we have a better chance of seeing all life in perspective — in unity.

John Muir a century ago said that if you pick up any part of the Universe you will find that it's hitched to every other part. We are still just beginning to learn all the implications of that prophetic statement. John Cobb and others, following the philosophy of Whitehead, tell us the same thing in what is now known as Process Theology.

Our efforts to conserve and to recycle and to respect the earth and all of its creatures and all its peoples has become an urgent agenda if humanity is to survive into the 21st Century. Already we have pushed the planet's life support systems to their very limits. The survival of the endangered species of animals and plants (and rain forests with their millions of species) always raises the old question: "Are they useful to me? Are they useful to man's economic exploitation? If not, then who cares?" We are now beginning to have enough vision to ask "Are they important in and for themselves, with as much right to exist as does the genus Homo Sapiens? Are they important for the balance of life and for the 'gene pool' of ongoing evolution? Are they going to be around for our grandchildren to have a right to ask these questions even if we don't?"

The vision of the unity of all of life, if we cherish it ourselves and share it with others, can make a difference. To cultivate this vision we don't even need to get out of our easy chairs or out of bed, but we do need to cultivate some new thought-patterns and put down some of our "traditional" assumptions and prejudices.

Thomas Berry, in his wonderful book The Dream of the Earth, gives substance and detail to this vision we need so much. He describes the planet itself (indeed the whole cosmos) as a living organism, interdependent and in a sense self-healing and self-actualizing. His vision can and must be widely shared. The future of life on earth depends on it!

Affirming Our Heritage

ONE OF THE NICE THINGS ABOUT GROWING OLDER is to enjoy and to affirm our heritage as a nation. I hope I am a loyal world citizen, and beyond that I affirm interdependence not only with the whole human family but with all creatures on Planet Earth.

I yield to no one in such a universal affirmation but also I yield to no one in my love for America — every rock and rill and templed hill, and every person of whatever race or creed. The older I grow the more I feel that this is above any political differences, serious as these often are.

Whenever I sing "O beautiful for pilgrim feet" I silently do honor to my Wiswall ancestor whose grave is in the Plymouth Burying Ground only a few feet from Miles Standish. And I honor Captain Noah Wiswall who was in the Revolutionary Army and wounded in action. I'm humbled and also proud of our Pilgrim heritage, which (in spite of their intolerance) laid the foundation for democracy and for freedom of worship in America.

Ten thousand heroes march within my blood.
Their life streams merge and bring mine to its flood.
My heart, be strong and steadfast, bold and true.
Ten thousands hearts have put their trust in you!

America has been blessed in so many ways, and we take them all too easily for granted. The richness and diversity of our natural resources, together with the diversity and the rich heritage of all the peoples now gathered in these fifty states, should be a source of gratitude for every one of us.

It's a peril that so many of the now generation seem to imply that "the past is a fink." That was the phrase one history professor used in decrying this attitude, and reminding us of the importance of knowing and appreciating our heritage. Let's take time to read some bits of our history. Let's continue to celebrate America and its possibilities. Let's cherish the best of our heritage and pass it on undiminished.

We Can All Do Something

ONE OF THE NICE THINGS ABOUT GROWING OLDER is to discover that, while we can't do everything any more, each one of us can still do something.

Historian Edmund Burke said that the greatest mistake people make is that since we can't do everything to right the wrongs of the world, we end up doing nothing. We need to remember the ancient Chinese proverb of hope: A journey of a thousand miles begins with a single step. To take that first step is often the hardest part of any big adventure.

I'm excited these days about the impact one person can make, and with very little effort, to save energy by recycling. To recycle one aluminum can saves enough energy to run the TV set for 3 hours. (It's because of the very high heat it takes to extract aluminum from bauxite ore, plus the great energy spent in mining and transporting the ore the first time round.) To recycle one glass jar or bottle saves enough energy to burn a 100 watt bulb for four hours. (Again it's because of the very high heat the first time sand is melted down to make glass, whereas remelting and remolding it takes much less energy.) To recycle a hundred or so pounds of newspaper saves cutting one tree in the forest to make the paper. And in the meanwhile, recycling also pays cash money!

What could one old lady, crippled and bedridden, do to change the world? The story goes back to the years when many churches were busy resettling refugees after World War II. A church in Arizona seemed to be setting the record for how many they took care of, and the national office thought they would try to find out how it was done. The answer? One person took the lead: she was so completely paralyzed that she had to dial the phone with a stylus held in her teeth, but she made hundreds of phone calls and it did the trick.

We can't do everything, but we oldsters can do something. And when we do, we become part of the answer instead of part of the problem!

Glimpsing The Citadel

ONE OF THE NICE THINGS ABOUT GROWING OLDER is to feel gratitude for the glimpses we have had along life's journey of the "New Jerusalem," the goal of brotherhood for the human family and for all creatures too. Every time we sing in our hearts we help to make real the prayer we all love:

> "O beautiful for patriot dream that sees beyond the years
> Thine alabaster cities gleam, undimmed by human tears."

John Bunyan was in a jail cell (as a Christian martyr) when he wrote the famous allegory of Pilgrim's Progress. At one point Pilgrim was mired down in the Slough of Despond and everything seemed hopeless. Then the mists opened and he saw a glimpse of the Celestial City beyond. At once it gave him new courage and strength to get out of the marsh — and the vision has given strength to many others also.

Dr. A.J. Cronin in The Citadel tells the story of an idealistic young doctor, reached at by the temptations of greed, glimpsing in the clouds at sunset the vision of that Citadel still luring him upward.

The legendary Harun al Raschid, inheriting the rule of a turbulent city, tried in vain to bring peace by establishing laws covering every detail of the life of his citizens. When that bogged down he hired a huge contingent of police to spy out offenders and enforce every law and so bring peace. That failed too. Finally he was inspired to seek artists and craftsmen who worked in secret in the palace to create an alabaster model of "the city which we are building together." One by one citizens and foreign traders also were brought into the palace by the young ruler himself, to view the "alabaster city gleaming." This vision finally did what more laws and more policemen could not do — it brought the citizens together to find peace at last through the goal and the promise they shared.

Isaiah's dream of the days when we shall beat our swords (and tanks and missiles) into plowshares may yet keep us alive long enough to bring it into reality.